The Elephant Hospital

by Kathy Darling

Photographs by Tara Darling

The Millbrook Press ● Brookfield, Connecticut

Published by The Millbrook Press, Inc.
2 Old New Milford Road
Brookfield, CT   06804
www.millbrookpress.com

Library of Congress Cataloging-in-Publication Data
Darling, Kathy.
The Elephant Hospital / by Kathy Darling ; photographs by Tara Darling.
p. cm.
Summary: Describes the work done by veterinarians at the Elephant Hospital in
Thailand, including helping pregnant and newborn elephants, elephants injured and
abused in logging operations, and elephants with illnesses and infections.
ISBN 0-7613-1723-6 (lib. bdg.)
I. Asiatic elephant—Diseases—Thailand—Juvenile literature. 2. Elephant Hospital
(Hang Chat, Thailand)—Juvenile literature. [I. Elephant Hospital (Hang Chat,
Thailand) 2. Asiatic elephant. 3. Elephants.] I. Darling, Tara, ill. II. Title.
SF997.5.E4 D37 2002   636.9'676—dc21   2001042103

The Elephant Hospital

How do you take care of a sick elephant?

You can't hear an elephant's heart with a veterinary stethoscope made for cows and horses. You can't give them shots, because regular-sized hypodermic needles aren't strong enough to pierce their two-inch-thick skin.

Animal doctors in Thailand had a giant problem. There are more than four thousand tame elephants in Thailand. The already endangered Asian elephants were dying because nobody knew how to take care of them when they were sick.

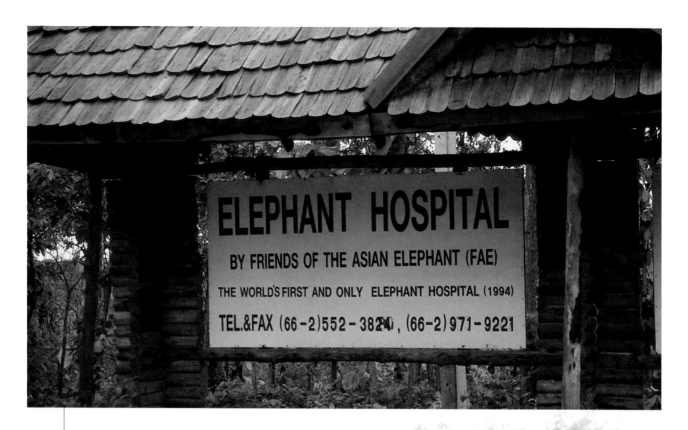

So, in 1994, with the help of the government of Thailand, veterinarians from around the world, and hundreds of volunteers who love the gray giants, the world's first Elephant Hospital was created in Lampang, Thailand. At last, there was an outdoor operating room—big enough for the biggest bulls. There was an X-ray machine that could take gigantic pictures, and a pharmacy that stocked pills the size of grapefruits.

Most of the elephant trainers, called mahouts, are very poor, so the doctors spread the word that there would be no charge for treatment. All elephants in need would be welcome. More than three hundred sick and injured elephants have made their way to the Elephant Hospital for help.

One of the things they do at the hospital is deliver giant babies! Giving birth to an elephant-sized baby is a big deal—even for a three-ton mother. Asian elephant cows aren't very speedy baby makers. In fact, they are pregnant longer than any other mammal, including their larger African elephant cousins. Their world-record pregnancy lasts about two years. It is hard to be more exact because a normal pregnancy can last as little as eighteen months or as long as twenty-five months.

The mother-elephant-to-be is not the only one who thinks that her baby's birth is a big deal. When a wild African or Asian elephant goes into labor, the other females in the herd form a protective circle around her. Known as "aunties," they will keep the newborn calf safe from lions, leopards, tigers—and from its own mother if necessary.

Oh, Baby!

It is often necessary. Elephants are good, even great, parents, but giving birth to a huge baby can cause so much pain that the new mother stomps around and hurts her newborn. If the aunties see that a mother cow is upset, they spring into action—moving the calf to safety, cleaning off the birth fluids, and cuddling it until the mother has calmed down.

Tame elephants don't always have companions who can act as aunties. That's why Auan was sent to the Elephant Hospital. She had lived at a temple where there weren't any other female elephants. During the birth of her first baby, the twenty-year-old mother panicked and killed it. So, at the end of her second pregnancy, she was sent to the Elephant Hospital where the doctors agreed to act as aunties.

As her second baby was being born, Auan panicked again. The veterinarians and mahouts were by her side but, without warning, the pain-crazed cow grabbed her baby, who was still inside the birth sac, and threw him into the air. When he fell to the ground, she stomped on him and bit his legs. Auan is stronger than fifty men, but the doctors and mahouts bravely faced her. Only by risking their own lives were they able to save the two-hundred-pound baby.

Auan and Pooh-pah Learn Together

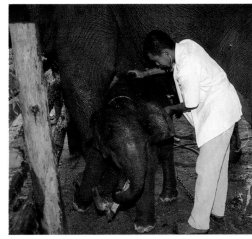

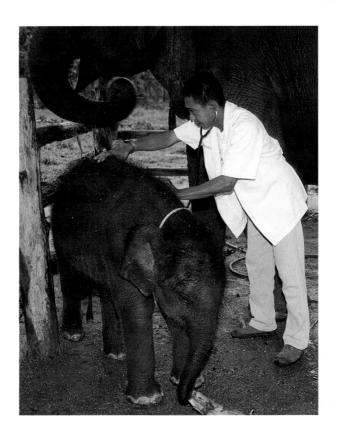

Auan's baby, Pooh-pah, was the first calf born at the Elephant Hospital. Because the vets were there to quickly pull him to safety, his injuries were not serious. You can see in these pictures, taken when he was three months old, that Pooh-pah is strong and healthy now and that Auan has become a good and gentle mother.

They do not have to go back to the temple because school-children in Thailand collected enough money to buy their freedom. One of the goals of the Elephant Hospital is to release captive elephants into a protected forest where they can live wild and free. Auan was born in the wild, and has been teaching Pooh-pah how to survive in a jungle. Every day she goes into the forest around the hospital to eat, and Pooh-pah tags along.

Milk is his main food and will be for at least three years, but the elephant child has begun to nibble on plants. Auan shows her adventurous son which foods are safe to eat and which are poisonous ones he must avoid. He has a lot to learn. Asian forests are full of dangerous plants—and animals. Auan has already had to rescue the curious calf from a deadly snake. His close encounter with a cobra is something that many baby and even some adult elephants don't survive.

Kamplai's Story

A few months after Pooh-pah's birth, the Elephant Hospital got another pregnant patient. Kamplai's owners sent her because they had heard about the hospital built for elephants and about the doctors who had saved Pooh-pah. Kamplai did not have a history of hurting babies like Auan did, but there weren't any other female elephants at the lumber camp where she worked.

For a month after Kamplai got to the Elephant Hospital, her mahouts fed her, and slept by her side, watching and waiting. On the night of the Thai New Year holiday called

Songkran, Kamplai went into labor. Frightened and in pain, the first-time mother didn't understand why she hurt so much. She began to trample everything around her. The mahouts and the veterinarians acted quickly and pulled the helpless newborn away from mom's big feet.

While one of the elephant doctors examined the calf to see if he was injured, another veterinarian gave Kamplai some medicine to ease her pain.

After a few hours the new mother had settled down and she began calling to her infant. He came—but with great difficulty. Usually, an elephant calf can walk when it is a couple of hours old, but walking, even standing, was a problem for this baby, who was named Songkran. He couldn't put any weight on one of his hind legs, which was red and swollen.

Songkran Gets Help

The hurt leg was not Songkran's only trouble. He was very tiny, weighing just a hundred pounds, which is barely half what a newborn elephant should weigh. But it was lack of height, not lack of weight, that was the calf's most serious problem. Songkran wasn't tall enough to reach Kamplai's nipples. Even when he stood on the tiptoes of his three uninjured legs, his mouth was still a long way from the life-giving milk. He could touch the nipples with his trunk, but an elephant calf can't nurse with its trunk. To drink, it has to put a nipple directly into its mouth.

Hour by hour, Songkran's cries for food grew weaker. Knowing he needed a hand, the vet aunties came to the rescue again. They showed the mahouts how to safely lift the injured calf and hold him close to one of the nipples in the cow's armpit so he could drink. It was important that Songkran get milk from his mother rather than a bottle because a cow's first day's milk, called colostrum, gives protection to the calf against some serious diseases.

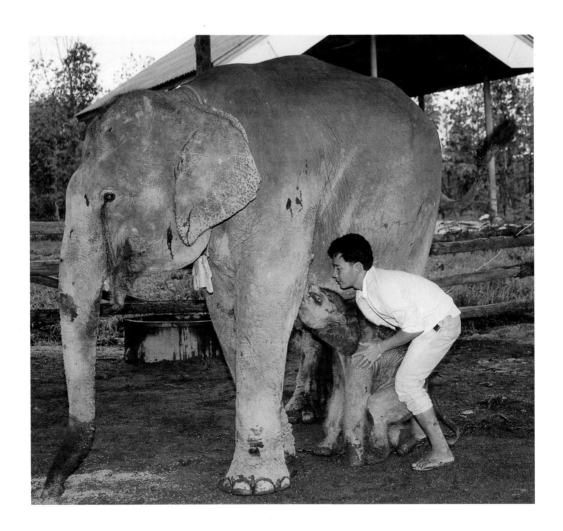

Kamplai knew her calf was having difficulty nursing and she figured out a way to help him. The solution was simple. She bent her knees. That first day she did a lot of bending. Her undersized son needed to suckle every two hours.

The next morning, Songkran was stronger, but his leg looked worse. The doctors had hoped it was only bruised but as the hot New Year's Day dawned they began to think that it might be broken. An X-ray picture proved it was. Songkran's broken leg would have to be put in a plaster cast—but it was too swollen. The problem was that the injured leg needed support immediately or it might get more damaged. The staff at the Elephant Hospital decided to put a temporary splint on the calf's leg.

You can't go out and buy an elephant splint, even a baby-sized one, so the vets made one. First they measured Songkran's leg. Then they gathered string and bamboo to make the splint, soft cotton to protect Songkran's leg, and adhesive to tape everything together. When the splint was ready, the doctors gathered a crew of helpers and headed down to the big open shed that serves as the emergency room of the Elephant Hospital.

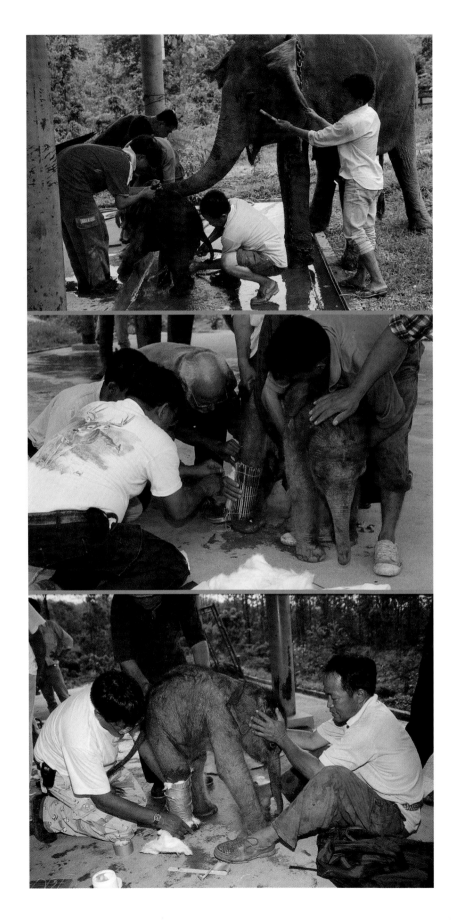

It was a good thing they rounded up a lot of helpers because it took six men to hold the wiggly little calf while the vets washed his leg and rubbed on a gooey, yellow, bacteria-killing ointment.

He continued to wiggle and wiggle while they wrapped his leg with the cotton padding. More than one of the elephant-wrestling helpers ended up underneath the baby, who thought the whole procedure was a fun game. A half hour passed before the doctors stuck the last bit of adhesive tape on the splinted leg.

19

When the swelling in Songkran's leg began to go down, his splint was replaced with a tighter fitting one. A few weeks later, the second splint was removed and a proper plaster cast was put on. Songkran's leg healed perfectly and he runs and plays with Pooh-pah now.

Four-Footed Lumberjacks

Hauling logs in a rain forest is a dangerous job. It has always been risky business—both for the men who cut the timber and for the elephants that drag the trees out of the forest. In the past ten years it has become even more hazardous. That's because logging is now illegal in most of Asia. The rain forests can no longer be logged or they will disappear. Anti-logging laws, however, have done little to stop the destruction. The cutting of the rain forests still goes on but now, to avoid getting caught, the "criminal" elephants and mahouts are forced to do the dangerous work at breakneck speed, sometimes even in the dark.

Because timber poaching is done in thick jungle far from any roads (or police), the elephants are not able to get medical care if they fall on a slippery slope, get caught in the logging chains, or are crushed by a tree. One out of every five logging elephants dies on the job each year.

Jungle work is also dangerous for an elephant veterinarian. Sick, injured, or just angry elephants can't always be controlled in the forest. They are as powerful as you would imagine and far quicker. A field vet must be both brave and athletic to do the job. "It pays to be careful," says Dr. Warakorn, one of the vets at the hospital. "Any sane person should be careful around an animal capable of pulling a good-sized tree out of the ground—especially if that animal is in pain."

A vet who isn't careful could get stabbed by an elephant's tusks, crushed by its forehead, punched with its three-hundred-pound trunk, bitten by its teeth, or kicked by its feet. Elephant attacks can include any combination of the above. Kicks are especially lethal, and elephants can deliver them in an astonishing variety. Both the front and back legs are able to kick away from or toward the body. Like a monster karate champion, an elephant can deliver a fatal blow three ways—forward, backward, or sideways. This elephant is using his trunk to swing a tree like a baseball bat.

This elephant had a fever and was cooling itself in the water. The doctor is checking to see if there is an infection that can be helped with medicine. First aid is easily given in the jungle but serious injuries are best treated back at the Elephant Hospital, near the laboratory and X-ray machines. The hospital has a giant truck to use as an elephant ambulance.

Kammee's Rescue

Kammee, a logger for most of her fifty-three years, was near death when she was loaded onto the elephant ambulance. Her cruel owner had worked her so long and hard that a chain harness had cut into the flesh of her chest and the wounds had become infected. The outlaw log poachers had beaten her and, even worse, had fed her drugs hidden in bananas so she would do more work. Kammee had been turned into a drug addict!

If she recovered from her wounds, Kammee would need to go through a detox program that the head veterinarian, Dr. Preecha, had created especially for addicted elephants. Before that could begin, Kammee needed an antibiotic to cure her infections. Penicillin doesn't come in elephant-sized pills so Dr. Warakorn gave her an injection. It isn't easy to give a shot to an animal with a tough two-inch-thick skin. (Elephants are sometimes called pachyderms, a name that means thick-skinned.)

First, the spot where the needle was to be inserted was cleaned with alcohol. Then, using two hands and plenty of muscle power, Dr. Warakorn stabbed the needle into Kammee's side. With the needle firmly in place, he filled a syringe with penicillin and attached it to the needle. Pushing the plunger was another two-handed job. Syringes may need to be refilled many times. To cure an elephant-sized infection, you need four hundred times as much antibiotic as you need for a human being.

Kammee had been neglected for a long time. She had worms, fleas, ticks, and lice. She got pills to kill the worms inside her and was dusted with powders that took care of the parasites on her skin.

After six months, most of Kammee's wounds were healed. But a few had formed abscesses that were full of pus. These stubborn sores needed a special treatment called a poultice. A poultice is a hot medicine that is applied directly to an injury. Dr. Warakorn had an excellent recipe for elephant poultice.

His assistant filled a pot with water and added garlic, chili peppers, herbs, grass, and tree bark and cooked it into a kind of medicine soup. When it was finished, he tied an old T-shirt onto a stick and soaked the medical mop in the hot poultice. Then he and Dr. Warakorn took turns slapping the wet T-shirt against the abscesses so that the hot medicine would soak in and heal the infection.

Ikhe's New Home

When Ikhe (pronounced eek-he) had a logging accident and broke her back leg, nobody took care of her. The bones healed so crookedly that she couldn't haul logs anymore. Nobody wanted a crippled elephant, and when she fell down a hill, she was left to die. Soldiers found her and called the Elephant Hospital. After a fifteen-hour drive, Ikhe reached the sanctuary of the Elephant Hospital. She was thin and had lots of small injuries, but she had found people who would heal her wounds and give her a home for life. The doctors cannot make her crooked leg straight but they have made it a bit better. It is amazing how fast Ikhe can walk with her crippled back leg. She likes to visit the other patients at the hospital and is always loving and gentle, especially to the babies.

Elephants on Parade

The Asian elephant lives longer than any mammal except human beings. A seventy-year life span is not unusual. This means that the problem of what to do with unemployed logging elephants, many of whom cannot be returned to the wild, will be around for many years to come. If they cannot find jobs, a lot of these loving, intelligent animals will be killed.

Long before the elephants were loggers they were pack animals, carrying people and cargo all across Asia. Tourists are giving them an opportunity to do that job again. Many former logging elephants have been gathered into camps that offer these rides.

An elephant-back ride through the jungle is thrilling. Seated ten feet above the ground, tourists get an elephant's-eye view of the forest and Thailand's historic ruins. Like a journey back in time, these special elephant rides allow people to imagine what these cities were like centuries ago. To make the ride more fun, the elephants are decorated in the traditional way with body painting and colorful silk costumes.

Some of the camps also have logging demonstrations. At the Elephant Conservation Center near the hospital, three of the calves give a painting show each week. Their colorful art is sold to raise money for elephant charities such as the Elephant Hospital.

An elephant
original by
Look Boc

Some of the money was used to buy a mobile unit for the Elephant Hospital. The traveling doctors are available twenty-four hours a day, seven days a week for emergencies. They also visits dozens of the camps to give routine care. The traveling docs vaccinate the loggers and performers against serious diseases, such as anthrax, tetanus, and elephant pox. Regular care includes a yearly dose of medicine to get rid of worms, especially the fatal heartworms, which are spread by the bites of mosquitoes and flies.

Fungal infections are commonly treated by the doctors. Asian rain forests are hot and steamy—perfect habitats for fungus. Like people, elephants get an infectious fungal disease called ringworm. On working elephants it often grows on their belly, under the constantly sweat-soaked straps that hold on their saddle. It is easy to see which animals have been treated for ringworm. The antifungal medicine used to treat it is bright purple.

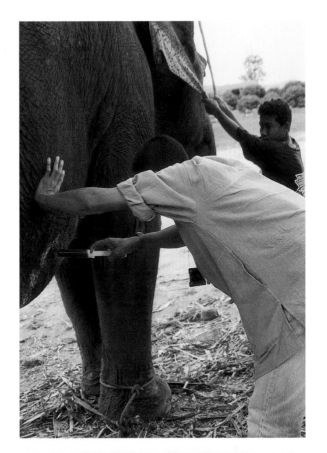

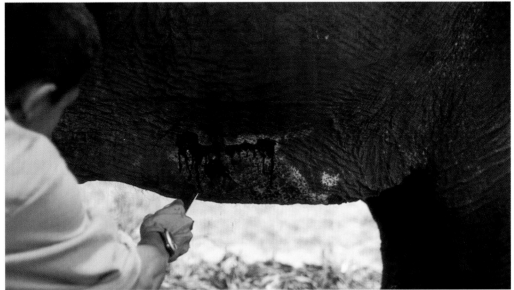

Danger Ahead

A lot of emergency calls are caused by musth, a strange state that male elephants go through every year. During the month or so that bulls spend in this sexually active condition, they are wild and aggressive. The musth-crazed elephants often fight and injure each other. These are the most dangerous cases for the vets to treat.

The area around the Thailand/Myanmar border has dangers of a different kind. There is a war going on. People get shot and so do elephants. The soldiers on both sides have also laid land mines in the forest. If an elephant steps on one, it gets a foot blown off. The doctors must sometimes go into these dangerous areas to treat the injured elephants. One of the land mine victims was saved and brought to the Elephant Hospital, where he is being fitted for an artificial foot.

The veterinarians' work is not all dangerous, though. Road trips have some nice parts too. The doctors, for instance, get to check out all the new babies born since their last visit. Each new calf gives them hope that a new generation of elephants will survive.

Would you like to know more about the Elephant Hospital? Or adopt an elephant in need? If so, become a member of the Friends of the Asian Elephant, the organization that sponsors the Elephant Hospital. The yearly membership fee is $24.00. You will get a membership card, a pin, and a quarterly newsletter.

E-mail address: fae@loxinfo.co.th

Mailing address: Friends of the Asian Elephant
                                350 Moo 8 Soi Ram
                                Indra 61, Ram Indra Road
                                Thareang, Bangkhen
                                Bangkok, Thailand   10230

Index